MW00834460

Happy Feet!

A Guide to Making Quilted Sneakers

BY JOAN BOBCHEK RADELL

ISBN: 979-8-218-29926-2

Yes, you can make quilted sneakers at home, with basic tools that are easily available. This guide will take you step-by-step through the process. It covers how to choose fabrics that are fun and functional, construction options, assembly, and finishing. There are plenty of photographs to help make each step easy to follow. We've included a section to help you source materials and tools. We highly recommend Bucklebee's Happy Feet! Sneaker Making Kit.

Please read through this guide before beginning the construction process. We'll offer tips, insight and guidance about fabric choices, interfacing, binding and hardware, and then jump into your quilted sneaker project on page 19. The supply list covers everything you will need to construct one pair of sneakers. You may have many items on the list on hand already. If there's an acceptable substitute, we'll note it. Sources for supplies are noted at the end of the guide.

Quilted Sneakers!

Whether you're a quilter, garment maker or crafter, you've probably made some unusual, surprising things. This guide will help you master yet another unexpected project to your list: quilted sneakers.

Our methods and techniques will result in professional results, but we'll let you in on a secret: this isn't a difficult project. Yes, you need to be precise; after all, you're making shoes and they have to fit. Shoe sizes are graded in small increments, so accuracy is important. But the sewing steps are straightforward and accessible to all but the most novice sewists, so don't be afraid to give this project a try. Resist the temptation to skip steps; we've tested our methods on many pair of shoes and many fabrics, and our simple method works beautifully and gives impressive results.

Don't let the word "quilted" intimidate you. Quilted Sneakers aren't a patchwork project requiring dozens of precision-cut pieces that need to be carefully assembled. We do use quilting related techniques, but don't fret if you've never made a quilt before. The finished shoes are comfortable, lightweight, and fun to wear. The pattern offers three options: a fun and funky ankle-bone height high-top; a basic, classic lace-up sneaker; and a low-rise lace-up sneaker that's summery and a bit dressier than a typical sneaker. The techniques used are the same for all three variations.

Choosing Your Fabrics

This guide is written for quilt-weight cotton fabrics, but any stable, tightly woven fabric will work well. Lightweight denim, chambray, lightweight cotton canvas, bottomweight linen, washable wool blends, and even some special occasion fabrics are good choices. Avoid knits, napped fabrics like flannel (they'll pill), or coated fabrics like oilcloth that don't breathe. Directional prints are fine to use. We recommend lining your sneakers with 100% cotton fabric for wearing comfort. If you use fabric other than cotton, be careful when fusing interfacings; use a pressing cloth and the appropriate heat setting for that fabric to avoid damaging your fabric and your iron. If you choose to use a special occasion fabric like satin brocade, lame or sequined fabric, it's a good idea to back it with an additional layer of featherweight interfacing or batiste. Use sew-in interfacings in this case, and a spritz of quilt basting spray to keep everything secure until you're ready to quilt the layers together. Sequined, beaded, and slippery fabrics won't accept quilting well; hand baste these to the backing support fabric from the wrong side at 1" intervals. Quilt the lining after fusing it to foam and woven interfacing, then use all-purpose spray adhesive to attach the backed-and-basted fancy fabric to the lining and support fabrics. Allow the adhesive to fully cure before sewing; follow the manufacturer's directions.

This project is a perfect showcase for those fat quarters you've stashed away for something special. You may opt for a contrast-

The word "sneaker" first appears in English in an 1887 educational journal, referring to students' rubber-soled shoes that allowed them to sneak up on their teachers. At the time, prison guards were also referred to as "sneaks" because of the rubber-soled shoes they wore, which dampened the sound of their footfalls.

ing tongue section; it's a fun detail that adds some spark to your step! Quilted sneakers get noticed, so don't be afraid to choose bright, eye-catching fabrics. Avoid very large prints; the motifs will lose their impact on such small component pieces. The largest focus motif shouldn't be larger than about 3 ½ inches across. Geometrics work beautifully, and make machine quilting quick and easy.

You can make patchwork sneakers. You'll need to construct the fabric for the exterior of your shoes, and then quilt it. Piece the equivalent of a fat quarter (18" x 22") for your uppers, keeping the following tips in mind. The surface area of the completed shoe is small, so plan for small, simple shapes. One-inch squares, 1 ½" flying geese, or 2" to 3" pieced blocks are all good choices. Foundation-piecing your patchwork makes working with tiny pieces much easier. Completely remove your foundation papers, or you'll hear crackles when you walk! It's tempting to try to make a focus block for the part of the upper that is right below your outer ankle bone. Because the upper has a curved lower edge, it's very difficult to get the placement perfect. Opt for an applique or other embellishment instead, unless you're up for quite a geometric challenge.

The easiest way to position a medallion-style single focus block is to foundation-piece it, and you'll have the best results if you've drafted foundations for small blocks before. You'll first make a paper tracing of the shoe upper pattern piece. Then you'll draw the position of your focus block exactly where you want it, glue-baste it to the foundation paper, and foundation piece the rest of the upper onto your traced pattern piece. Remember to flip the pattern piece over when you draft the foundation lines for the other shoe! When assembled, the lower edge of the shoe upper has a gentle curve. Position any specialty blocks parallel to this lower edge.

If you want to embellish your sneakers with embroidery, applique, or rhinestones, plan on doing this work after the uppers are bound and ready to attach to the soles. Use prong-set, not heat set, gemstones for durability. If you want to paint your sneakers, choose an acrylic paint that is flexible when dry. There are acrylic shoe paints made expressly for this purpose. They're available from several online retailers.

Fussy Cutting and Pattern Placement

You may find that your fabric has an ideal motif for the toe of your sneakers. Keep in mind that the rounded toe edge will extend into the sole by about ½". Use a fabric marker or chalk to trace around your tongue piece when you've found the exact placement you want on the fabric. Cut out this piece leaving a very wide margin— at least ¾" on all edges. Find the motif again on your fabric, and stack your first cut tongue piece on top of it, matching the print around the edges as perfectly as you can. Using this piece as a pattern, cut out your second piece of fabric for the second tongue. Flip your tongue pattern piece over (it's not symmetrical!) and trace around it, mirroring your first piece as best you can.

If you are using a directional print, be careful to position your pattern pieces so that the fabric's print is facing in the correct direction. Flowers grow upwards! Directional prints on the tongue usually look best flowing upward from toe to the ankle, but check to make sure that choice is the best for your particular fabric. In the cover illustration, for instance, the fabric is running from the ankle down to the toe.

Some prints look especially good when the print travels attractively around the shoe. Take the time to audition fabric placement. Use the fabric to its best advantage. You might need a bit more yardage for some prints if you want both shoes to be identical.

A cobbler repairs or refurbishes shoes; a cordwainer makes new shoes from new leather. The word "cordwainer" derives from the city of Cordoba, Spain, famed for its beautiful cordovan goat-leather that was used in the finest shoes.

Thread

This project has four major sewing steps: quilting your fabric, machine basting the cut edges, applying binding, and joining the back dart. We prefer size 40 cotton thread for quilting lines, and a fairly short 2.2 stitch length. Size 50 cotton or all-purpose polyester thread is a good size for the other sewing tasks.

Take your time when you choose your quilting thread color. Do you want your quilting lines to show? If not, choose a thread that blends well, or is the color of the print background. If so, decide which color or colors will best accent your exterior fabric choice. Think about the bobbin thread, too! This is a great project for variegated quilting thread. It's a subtle highlight that can add impact.

Most sneaker kits are packed with heavily-waxed fine cord that matches the sole color. But shoemaking threads come in lots of colors. Think about using a coordinating color instead of black or white, or matching your cord color to the color of your binding.

Protecting and Cleaning

You might want to consider a waterproofing or stainproofing spray treatment. Don't use brush-on waterproofers; they'll completely seal the minuscule gaps in the fabric and your sneakers will be hot and uncomfortable. Choose a product designed for lightweight, indoor fabric. You can opt to spot clean your sneakers with a method appropriate for the fabric you've used, as well. There's no need to use a fabric protectant on the lining; your sneakers will be more comfortable if you let that lining breathe. Scuff marks on the sidewalls of white soles can be easily cleaned with a small soft brush. A soft child's toothbrush is perfect for the job. Use a drop of dish soap, and a little warm water. You can protect your shoes during storage or travel by slipping sole protectors or even a shower cap over them. Because they're lightweight and so comfortable, quilted sneakers are delightful travel companions and always a great conversation starter.

Interfacing

Our guide calls for a medium-weight woven interfacing and a fusible foam interlining. They form the support structure for your fantastic fashion fabrics. The woven fusible interfacing stabilizes your exterior fabrics, and allows your sneakers to keep their smooth, professional finish. Unwoven interfacing tends to soften over time, so woven is the better choice.

If you choose to use batting instead of fusible foam, your sneakers will quickly lose their crisp shape and become saggy and sad. The fusible foam is breathable and very comfortable to wear. Different brands of fusible foam have different thicknesses and rigidity, with Pellon brand being the beefiest, and Annie's Soft-N-Stable the softest. Bosal In-R-Form is in the middle, toward the stiffer end of the spectrum. We prefer stiffer foam for high tops, especially.

Take the time to fuse your fabrics with care. Using a barely damp pressing cloth, a low cotton setting on your dry iron and very firm pressure, fuse from the center of your fabric sandwich toward the outer edges in all directions. If your pressing cloth dries out, re-dampen it as you work. Use an up-and-down pressing motion; don't iron back-and-forth. The heat from your iron melts the adhesive on your interfacings; the pressure you apply makes the interfacing adhere to the back of your fabrics. If you use a tradi-tional back-and-forth motion, your fabrics may slip and tiny wrin-kles and tucks are almost inevitable. An overhand fabric press works well for fusing, if you have access to one. Allow your fabric to cool on a flat surface. If you see bubbles or unfused sections, use a little steam to re-press. If you take the time to fuse your fabrics properly, quilting your fabric sandwich is a breeze!

Quilting

This instructions in this guide will tell you to quilt your fabrics in a one-inch grid, but there are several things to consider that might influence the way you quilt your fabrics together. If your fabric is a stripe or geometric print, it might be easier and more attractive to quilt using the fabric print as a guide instead of a grid. If your fabric is woven more loosely than quilting cotton, you'll want quilting lines that are a bit closer together than 1". Mark your quilting lines with a removable chalk-based fabric marker, painter's tape, or use a quilting bar if your machine or walking-foot assembly offers one. There's no need for fancy quilting; high-impact fabrics with simple quilting works best.

Do you need to quilt in a square grid? No! Consider a serpentine stitch, a simple decorative stitch, channel quilting, or matchstick quilting. Just make sure your quilting lines are no more than 1" apart. Not only does this keep layers from shifting from the handling you'll give them during construction and later during normal wear; you'll find that the close quilting lines help the shoe keep its structured shape over time.

If you make your sneakers in a solid color, or in a print that reads as a solid, your quilting lines will be very visible. To minimize visibility use a thread color that matches the fabric color, but think about using your quilting lines as a design detail. Bright red quilting on a navy blue tonal, metallic silver quilting on jet black, or variegated autumn colors quilted on a soft green batik would all look great!

Prepping Uppers for Attachments

The sneaker's upper components are attached to the soles with hand-stitching. The guide will give detailed instructions on this step; if you follow them exactly everything will line up just right and your shoes will be secure and ready to wear. You'll be punching a lot of holes in your prepped fabric. It's tempting to skip the attachment hole-punching step, but the hole placement marks on the pattern and the stitch placement marks on the sole are designed to match up perfectly. A saddler's needle doesn't have a sharp point, so working it through two layers of fabric, a layer of interfacing and a layer of foam is no easy task. Take a few minutes to punch the holes. An ultra fine point Sharpie and a light touch is the best way to mark hole placement, unless your fabric is very dark. It doesn't matter if you mark on the exterior or the lining; the marks will be covered by the insoles. Mark on the side that is most visible. You can use a hand punch and hammer, a pliers-type leather punch, or a hollow-point hole punch and hammer. Your holes should be 2mm or a little less. We recommend putting the tiniest drop of seam sealant like Fray-Check on every hole on both the exterior and lining sides. The fusible interfacing adhesive does minimize fraying, but a little extra insurance doesn't hurt!

Try your best not to break your quilting threads as you punch your sewing (and eyelet holes in a later step). If you have to shift the hole placement a few threads in either direction to keep from cutting quilting lines, that's fine. If you do cut them, you can use permanent flexible fabric glue to seal the cut ends to the fabric. Apply a tiny drop with an old machine needle and work it into the fibers of the fabric as well as the cut ends of the threads. Apply pressure with the tip of the needle until the cut thread ends stay put.

Binding

Your binding is a great way to add a little bit of surprise color to your shoes. If you're using neutrals, consider a jewel-tone; the binding finishes at a mere ¼" so rich colors won't overwhelm your exterior fabrics. Because some of the turns are tight, especially on the tongue sections, you must use bias binding for a smooth finish. You'll need four pieces of 1 ¾" wide binding; you may have to piece your bias to get the lengths you need. Join binding piec-

Semi-pro basketballer Charles Taylor had nothing to do with the design of iconic Converse All-Star high-top sneakers. He was a traveling salesman who was so successful at promoting the shoes in the 1920s that the Converse company added his signature to the medallion on the ankle of the shoes. They've been affectionately called Chuck Taylors ever since.

es with a diagonal seam to minimize bulk. Press the seam open with a hot, dry iron, then press the strip in half lengthwise.

The idea of working with a very narrow binding can be intimidating. Our guide calls for 1.75" bias binding; handle it gently to avoid stretching it out of shape. Prep it properly: fold it exactly in half and press it very well with a dry iron without stretching it. You may pre-shape the bias tape by matching the raw edges and steam pressing it along the edge of your shoe components before sewing it in place. This pre-shaping doesn't have to be exact; it just gives the tape a nudge in the direction that you want it to go as you sew. Always sew your bias binding to the lining side of the upper and tongue. Press again, using the side of the iron to push the binding firmly away from the seam. Flip your piece over, fold the binding over the raw edge and press in place. Use fabric clips or ⅛" double stick tape to hold the binding firm and steady as you topstitch it down. Sew at an even, medium speed right along the fold, using a slightly shortened stitch length for the smoothest, most professional curves. After you've topstitched, press the component again. Yes, there's a lot of pressing involved, but don't skip it — all that pressing is the secret to professional results.

There's another binding option to consider: fold-over elastic, sometimes called lingerie elastic. It's a product that works well for binding curves. It comes in a wide variety of colors, has a pretty sheen and it's inexpensive. Use the ⅝" width and sew it to the lining side of the components shiny side down, stretching very gently. Fold it over to the right side, secure with clips or ⅛" double-faced tape, and topstitch in place. This method takes a bit of practice but gives an excellent result; try it on scraps first until you're comfortable.

Eyelets

Use eyelets as an accent color! Although we tend to think of traditional metallics, eyelets are available in so many colors that it's easy to find one that really sets your fabric off. Eyelets are available in reasonably-priced kits that include the setting tool and anvil that you'll need to apply them. You'll need two piece eyelets that measure $^3/_{16}$" on the inside diameter. Two piece eyelets set smoothly with no rough edges that can snag on your shoelaces. Most eyelets with $^3/_{16}$" holes are ⅜" across in total, but read the product description carefully before you purchase them, and don't punch your eyelet holes until you're ready to set them in just in case of a size discrepancy. Set a couple of practice eyelets in scrap fabrics before setting them into your shoes to master just how hard to whack! your hammer for a perfect set. Remember that your lining should be facing you when you're setting eyelets — check twice! Eyelets set in upside down are very, very difficult to remove. If you do make an error and need to remove an eyelet, we've found that a pair of small, wide-jawed nippers are the best tool to use. Work the jaws of the nippers under the rim of the top side of the eyelet, and squeeze it out-of-round. Flip the piece over and repeat on the washer side of the eyelet. Repeat this sequence until the eyelet is loose enough to remove. While you're doing this, be very, very careful not to damage the fabric or the quilting threads. Slow and steady is the key to success. A tiny, tiny drop of flexible permanent fabric glue applied with the tip of a stiletto can fix a few frayed or errant threads before you reset the eyelet properly.

Hand Sewing

Each shoe is finished by handsewing the upper components to the sole. The heavy waxed cord used is designed specifically for shoemaking; it's abrasion resistant, strong, and easy to work with because it has a minimal twist. Each shoe will take about 3 ½ yards of cord, depending on size of course. Handwaxed upholstery or buttonhole thread is not an appropriate substitute; the correct cord is easy to find and inexpensive. A heavy-duty thimble will make the hand-sewing much more comfortable. If you need to remove stitches — it happens! — unthread your needle and pull the errant stitches out one at a time. Rethread your needle and resew correctly. It can be tricky to sew the toe portion of the upper because it's an enclosed and dark space. A penlight comes in very handy if you can't find your punched holes. Pull your stitches tight, but no so tightly that the upper edge of the sidewall of the sole gets wavy. When both passes of handsewing are complete, you'll be surprised at how well the uppers fit into the soles. You should just barely be able to slip a fingernail between the fabric and the edge of the sole.

In 1952, Adidas founder Adi Dassler bought the now-legendary "three stripe" logo from a Finnish athletic shoe company. The price? $1,750 and two bottles of whisky.

In general, 3 ½ yards of cord will complete one shoe — more for larger sizes, less for smaller. If your cord is too short to complete the entire handsewing process with one length, just leave a 3" tail on the old cord, and start the new cord leaving a 3" tail. When you've completed the handsewing on that sneaker, snug up the ending and beginning stitches, tie the tails together tightly, and clip them off. Leave about half an inch of the tails unclipped, and put a tiny drop of seam sealant or permanent fabric glue on the knot.

Insoles

The insoles that come with most sole kits are thick, padded, comfortable and very well made. Everyone is different, of course, and they may not be right for you. You can use any insole you'd like in your sneakers. You may have to do a bit of trimming, but the provided insoles make a great pattern! Keep in mind that the insoles are designed to cover your handsewing stitches; other brands and styles of insole may not be thick enough to cover the stitching. If you wear custom orthotics or arch supports, they'll fit into your sneaker without a problem.

Should you glue your insoles down? This is truly up to you. We leave ours unglued and have had no issues at all with slipping or bunching. The insoles can be removed, replaced, or reused. If you choose to glue your insoles down, use a permanent glue designed for shoemaking. (Shoe-Goo is a widely-available brand.) These glues are engineered to hold up to flexion and moisture over time. Remember that less is more when gluing, and follow all of the glue manufacturer's instructions.

Reusing Soles

You can deconstruct your sneakers and reuse soles and insoles. Remove the insole and use the tips of sharp scissors or thread nippers to clip every other stitch on the inside. Around the toe of the shoe, you'll need to clip on the outside; use a stiletto or other thin, sturdy tool to lift your stitch away from the sole itself before clipping. Pull the clipped stitches, then repeat the clipping/pulling process on the remaining hand stitches. Remove both sections of the uppers, clean your soles, and they're ready to reuse. You can reuse the insoles as well; if they're extremely worn or dirty, replace them with commercial insoles.

General sewing tips

- Use a size 90 sharp or microtex needle. A universal-point needle is not sharp enough to pierce the fusible foam easily.

- All seam allowances are ¼" unless the instructions say otherwise.

- Use a 2.6 to 2.8 stitch length for quilting lines. Use a 2.2 stitch length for your bindings.

- A quarter-inch presser foot without a flange or "wall" is helpful for construction. Use a wide-toed presser foot for good visibility for quilting lines. A quilting bar is very useful as well.

- If your machine has an even-feed feature, use it. A walking-foot attachment is very helpful if your machine doesn't have even-feed options.

- Sew curves at a steady slow-to-medium speed.

- Sew stabilizing stitches around the edges of each component piece within the ¼" seam allowance.

General pressing tips

- The success of this project depends heavily on great pressing. Don't rely on finger-pressing or a seam roller. Use a dry iron and a fine spray water bottle to control the application of steam where instructed.

- These instructions are written for cotton fabrics. If you're using a different fiber content, use the heat setting on your iron that's appropriate for that fabric. Always test on scraps first!

General pattern prep tips

If you are printing your own pattern; make sure you choose the "Actual Size" option in your printer options. It's very, very important to check the 4" line on the pattern sheet with a ruler to make sure your pattern is accurate. The most accurate printing results are achieved by printing from a laptop or desktop computer rather than a mobile device. We've found that $^1/_{16}$" variance or less is inconsequential. If your printed pattern is off by more than that, your shoes will not fit comfortably! Make adjustments in 1% increments if necessary and reprint. Photographs in this guide show the hi-top sneaker. There are no differences in construction should you choose the classic or ultra-low option.

On first glance, both the complete upper pattern and the tongue pattern appear symmetrical. But if you look closely, you'll see that the outer side of the uppers have one more support-row stitching hole than the inner side, and that the outer side (marked with a notch for easy identification) of the tongue is longer than the inner side. These differences, although subtle, allow the shoe to fit comfortably and smoothly over your foot and add extra reinforcement to the sneaker where it will naturally bend with each step. Mark the lining of the uppers at the center back, near the bottom edge by the dart, with a small uppercase L or R; mark the lining of the toes at the very tip of the toe curve as well. These marks will be covered by the insole, so they won't show.

If you're ready for an out-of-the ordinary, showstopping project, let's get started!

Instructions

You may opt to make the exterior of your sneakers out of a single fabric, two fabrics, or three. The cover photo shows the three fabric option.

Single Fabric Option—all components are cut from the same fabric:

- ½ yard of quilt weight cotton for upper, tongue, and binding
- ¼ yard of quilt weight cotton for lining; Fat Quarter preferred (18" x 22")

Cut 4 pieces of of 1.75" wide bias strips, about 18" long. *You may have to join your binding pieces. Use a diagonal seam to join binding pieces, press seam allowances open.*

Two Fabric Option—uppers from one fabric, contrast tongue and binding:

- ¼ yard of quilt weight cotton for upper; Fat Quarter preferred
- ¼ yard of quilt weight cotton for lining; Fat Quarter preferred (18" x 22")
- ¼ yard of quilt weight cotton for tongue and binding

Cut 4 pieces of of 1.75" wide bias strips, about 18" long. *You may have to join your binding pieces. Use a diagonal seam to join binding pieces, press seam allowances open.*

Three Fabric Option—uppers from one fabric, contrast tongue, contrast binding:

- ¼ of quilt weight cotton for upper; Fat Quarter preferred (18" x 22")
- Quilt weight cotton for tongue; 10" square is plenty
- ¼ yard of quilt weight cotton for lining; Fat Quarter preferred (18" x 22")

Cut 4 pieces of of 1.75" wide bias strips, about 18" long. *You may have to join your binding pieces. Use a diagonal seam to join binding pieces, press seam allowances open.* Use a Fat Quarter, scrap fabric, or yardage as you prefer.

Materials Needed for All Options:

Items included in Bucklebee Sneaker Kit are in **red**. A source list is included at the end of this guide.

- ½ yard double sided fusible foam interlining (Bosal In-R-Form, Soft 'n' Stable by Annie's, and Pellon Flex-Foam Ff79F2 are all great choices and readily available at fabric stores or from online retailers.)
- ½ yard midweight woven fusible interfacing (We recommend Pellon SF101)

Note: These interfacing/interlinings give the shoes their structure. If you substitute other interfacings, quilt batting, or omit interfacing/interlining altogether, your shoes will be very soft and shapeless, like slippers.

- **6–7 yards of heavy, waxed leatherworking cord, sometimes called "artificial sinew."** It's heavily waxed to add strength, abrasion resistance and to keep it from tangling as you use it.

- A long, sharp needle with a large eye, about 3" long, OR a very sharp awl or sharp stiletto.

- **A size 4 saddler's needle.** This is optional, but it makes assembling the sneakers so much easier that it's worth having. A saddler's needle is heavy, with a medium eye, straight shaft, and rounded tip.

- A 2mm leather punch, or a rotary leather punch with a 2mm die.

- $3/8$" two-part eyelets, and setting tools, and a hammer or jeweler's mallet. The interior diameter of the eyelet should be $3/16$". These are available at online retailers and leatherworking shops. Usually, the eyelets are packaged in a kit with setting tools: a special anvil and setter. You'll need 32 eyelet sets for hi-tops; fewer for classic or ultra-low. Do not purchase single-piece eyelets; they'll pull through the fabric and chew through your shoelaces. Look for a two-part eyelet with an eyelet that shows on the exterior side and a small round washer that fits on the lining side of your shoe. Eyelets are available in lots of different colors.

- **A hard thimble**: metal, leather, or PVC

- Sewing thread to match or coordinate with your fabrics. Use cotton thread for quilting, and cotton or polyester thread for construction.

- One pair of shoelaces to match, contrast or coordinate with your exterior fabrics. Hi-tops require 60" laces; classic and ultra low sneakers use 45" laces.

- Sharp sewing scissors, rotary cutting supplies optional

- About 20 small fabric clips or very small binder clips. We find $1/8$" fabric clips are ideal.

- Sewing machine in good working order. You'll need a bobbin for your quilting thread and one for general construction thread.

- Seam sealant, such as Fray-Check. Optional: permanent flexible fabric glue.

- Optional: Permanent ultra-flexible shoemaking glue, such as Shoo-Goo for permanently attaching insoles to the sole bed.

- Basic sewing supplies

- Iron and ironing board or pressing surface.

- **Sneaker pattern.** If you need to download a copy of the pattern, go to https://www.sneakerkit.eu/c-3526931/patterns. Download the "Classic 3-in-1" in the size that corresponds to your soles. When printing, make certain you've set your printer to "Actual Size" and double check the 4" line on the pattern to make sure your pattern is the correct size. Otherwise, your shoes won't fit!

Cut your fabrics according to the fabric option you've chosen. If the chart indicates "for all options," make sure you cut that piece as well.

COMPONENT	CUT	SIZE	NOTES
Fusible Foam for all options	1	18" x 22"	
Fusible Foam for 2- or 3-fabric option	1	5" x 20"	
Fusible Interfacing for all options	1	18" x 22"	Some SF101 is only 20" wide. Use an 18" cut. If you're using a wider product, cut as indicated in the chart.
Fusible Interfacing for 2- or 3-fabric option	1	5" x 20"	
Lining Fabric for all options	1	18" x 22"	
Exterior Fabric for 1-fabric option	1	18" x 22"	
Exterior Fabric for 2- or 3-fabric option, uppers	1	18" x 22"	
Exterior Fabric for 2- or 3-fabric option, tongue	1	5" x 22"	

Step 1: Quilt your fabrics

For the uppers: Make sure your fat-quarter fabrics are well pressed and wrinkle free. Lay your lining fabric right side DOWN on your pressing surface. On top of that lay your fusible foam, matching raw edges (they may not match perfectly, that's okay.) On top of that, lay your fusible interfacing fusible side UP, again matching the raw edges. If they don't match exactly, split the difference and do your best to center your interfacing on the foam. Finally, lay your exterior fabric right side UP on top of the fusible interfacing. Smooth this sandwich from the center out with long, sweeping hand motions. Set your iron to the cotton setting; DO NOT use the highest heat setting. Cover the quilt sandwich with a lightly but evenly dampened pressing cloth. Place your iron in the center of the stack, and press down, hard, for about 5 seconds. Working from the center to the outer edges, smoothing as you go, continue to press in 5 second increments. Do NOT iron back and forth; use an up-and-down motion only. When the whole piece is fused, smooth the fabric from the center outward in long, medium pressure, even strokes. Flip the piece over and repeat the smoothing step. Allow to cool flat for a minute or two before proceeding to the next step. Make sure you check for any tiny folds, pleats or tucks, and correct those before quilting.

Using a long ruler, mark a line from short side to short side parallel to the long edge of your fabric. Use a light touch with a removable fabric marker or chalk. Mark a line perpendicular to the first line from long side to long side. These will be your first two quilting lines. Using a 2.6–2.8 stitch length and a walking foot or even-feed feature, quilt these two lines first. Quilt the whole sandwich in a 1" grid pattern, using a quilting bar, painter's tape, or other marking system to keep your stitching lines even and straight.

Two or Three Fabric Option ONLY: For the tongue: Layer your 5" x 20" fabrics, foam, and interfacing in the same order and direction as you did for the uppers. Fuse. Mark a line down the center of the center of the fused fabrics in both directions, taking care to make sure they're perpendicular to each other. Quilt in a 1" grid.

Press all quilted pieces with a little steam. If you find any tiny tucks in your quilting lines, worth them out carefully with the tip of your iron and a spritz of water.

Step 2: Cut your uppers and tongues

After printing and checking that your pattern pieces are the correct size, trim your pattern pieces exactly on the cutting line. You may want to laminate your pattern pieces, or cover them with clear shelf liner. Trim away all of the laminating plastic. Tape your upper patterns together where indicated on the pattern. (Tip: leave a tab extension along the taping line on one pattern piece when cutting out your pattern. Use this to support your taped joint.) Clip the marking notch on the lower edge of the upper pattern. Your joined, completed pattern piece will resemble a long banana.

Using a 2mm punch and hammer, and working on a protective surface (an old cutting board works well for this), punch a tiny hole through each dot along the long sides of the upper pattern, and along the front curve of the tongue. Notice that near the front, there's a double row of holes. Make sure your punch through all of them. **DO NOT punch out the two holes on the front edges of the upper pattern, and the four holes on the side edges of the tongue pattern. These holes are for leatherworking only.**

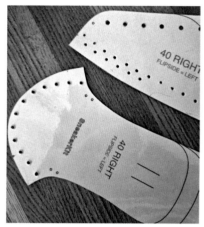

For the single fabric option, use this pattern layout guide:

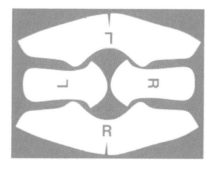

For the double or triple fabric options, follow these cutting instructions — Using your quilting lines as a guide, and keeping the direction and layout of the print of your fabric in mind, lay your prepped upper pattern on your large piece of quilted fabric. Using a removable fabric marker, trace around the outside of your pattern piece. This is the upper for your right shoe. Flip your pattern piece over, and repeat the process; this is the upper for your left shoe. Cut out both pieces carefully on your traced line. Mark which side is the right shoe next to the open dart on the lining side.

With the right side up, lay your pattern over the right upper. Using a fine-tipped marker (a Sharpie is the best marking tool for this), make a mark through each of your punched holes. Using a 2mm punch, punch a hole through all fabric layers at each dot along the bottom edge of the piece. Notice that near the front, there's a double row of holes. Make sure you punch through all of them. Flip your pattern piece over, and repeat for the left upper. *Note: Try to avoid punching through your quilting lines. If you have a shift a teeny bit to either side to keep from cutting quilting, that's okay.*

Center your tongue pattern piece over your remaining piece of 5" x 20" quilted fabric. Make sure that the center line of quilting is centered under the pattern piece. Trace around the pattern piece, mark the tiny holes, and punch out the holes just as you did for the uppers.

Edgestitch around all four shoe pieces, ⅛" from the raw edges. This stablizes the edge of the fabric. If your fabric is more loosely woven than quilting cotton, like linen or cotton canvas, use a narrow zig-zag stitch instead of a straight stitch. This edgestitching also compresses the edge of the foam interlining, making it easier to apply your binding.

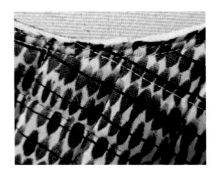

Step 3: Bind your uppers and tongues

Carefully press your binding strips in half lengthwise. Starting from the center back and working toward the outer edges, clip your binding strips to the upper edge of the lining side of the right shoe upper, matching raw edges. Handle the binding carefully.

From the lining side, using a scant ¼" seam allowance, sew your binding in place. Press outward, making sure your binding is pressed all the way out and that there aren't any tucks or pleats along the seamline.

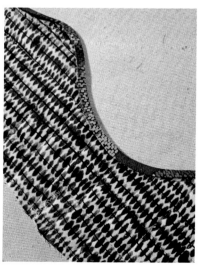

Trim the shoe upper piece ONLY, not the binding, to just over ⅛" along any curves in the edge. Try not to cut through your edgestitching. Fold the binding to the right side evenly and smoothly, and press in place so that it just covers the seam you just stitched. Take your time!

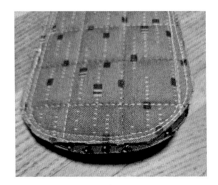

Use clips or sections of ⅛" double stick tape to hold the binding in place as you position it. Edgestitch the binding in place. For the best results, sew slowly and evenly, avoiding starts and stops if you can. Press well. Repeat for the remaining three shoe components. When binding the tongue, you'll have sharper curves to navigate. Use a shorter stitch length and sew at an even speed. You may need a little steam to help settle the binding smoothly in place. Remember to sew your binding to the LINING side, and finish on the RIGHT side.

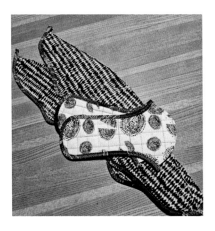

Step 4: Complete the uppers

In the center back of each upper, there's a dart. Put the tip of the dart triangle flat under your presser foot. With both hands, pull the dart closed, just until the cut edges butt up against each other. Using a medium zig-zag stitch, join the edges of the dart. Backstitch at each end of this little seam.

Using a 4mm or ⁵/₁₆" punch, or a paper punch, punch out each of the eyelet holes of your upper pattern, on the left and on the right. Lay your right upper flat on your work surface, right side up. Lay your prepped pattern piece on top of the right-hand side of your bound upper, matching the upper edge of the binding to the upper edge of the pattern. It may not match exactly; the important thing to keep in mind is that your row of eyelets should be straight and even along the front edge of the shoe. When you've got your pattern positioned correctly, mark each eyelet hole with a removable fabric marker. Mark the right-hand side only! Use your punch to punch out each eyelet hole. Fold the upper in half, lining side facing out, matching the bound edges. Mark the eyelet holes through the holes you just punched on the left side of the piece. Open the piece up and make sure everything looks even. Punch the holes in the left side. Note: Try to avoid punching through your quilting lines. If you have a shift a teeny bit to either side to keep from cutting quilting, that's okay.

Repeat for the left upper. Remember to flip your pattern piece upside down! Alternatively, you can use your right upper to mark the holes on your left upper; just make sure you mark the hole positions with the uppers right side together.

Put a very small drop of seam sealant on the edges of each punched eyelet hole. If you've cut through a quilting line, use a pin or your stiletto to lay the cut end of the thread straight and flat and secure with a tiny drop of permanent fabric glue. With luck, you can catch it under the eyelet edges to keep it from coming unsewn. You may prefer to re-sew that particular quilting line. Backstitch at the eyelet end of the line.

Each ⅜" eyelet has two parts; the eyelet itself and a thin metal washer. The setting kit has an anvil with a little post in the center, and a striker with a hole drilled in one end. Drop an eyelet onto the post of the anvil, pretty side down. Slip your fabric RIGHT SIDE DOWN over the eyelet; you should be able to see the eyelet edges clearly. Press the fabric down around the shaft of the eyelet if you need to. Thread the washer onto the anvil post so that the edges of the eyelet come

up through it. Set the striker onto the post, and give it a firm whack with the hammer. Check to make sure that the edges of the eyelet have curled smoothly around the inner edge of the washer. If there's a raised or rough spot, put the work back on the anvil and give it another whack. Install all the eyelets on the right upper, then repeat for the left.

It's VERY hard to remove an eyelet once it's been installed, so check twice before putting a hammer to the striker. If you do make an error and need to remove an eyelet, we've found that a pair of small, wide-jawed nippers are the best tool to use. Work the jaws of the nippers under the rim of the top side of the eyelet, and squeeze it out-of-round. Flip the piece over and repeat on the washer side of the eyelet. Repeat this sequence until the eyelet is loose enough to remove. While you're doing this, be very, very careful not to damage the fabric or the quilting threads. Slow and steady is the key to success. A tiny, tiny drop of flexible permanent fabric glue applied with the tip of a stiletto can fix a few frayed or errant threads before you reset the eyelet properly.

Step 5: Assemble the shoes

With a sharp stiletto, awl, or heavy needle, punch through every little hole marked on both sneaker soles. Prepping the sewing holes in this way makes assembly much, much easier, so don't skip this step.

Make sure you can find the little notch on the bottom raw edge of your uppers. If not, use the pattern to re-locate it and mark it.

Thread 4 yards of waxed shoemaking cord onto a saddler's needle. The lightly twisted cord is heavily waxed, so that it rarely tangles and doesn't fray when used. Take the insole out of the right shoe sole. On the inside of the sole, along the left standing edge near the heel, look for an upward arrow embossed into the sole itself. This is where you'll begin sewing.

Working from the inside of the sole, insert your needle through the hole at the notch marking on your right upper, then push it though the hole at the arrow. Pull the cord through, leaving a 4" tail. Working toward the heel, push your needle through the next hole on the sole from the outside toward the inside of the shoe,and then through the next punched hole on the upper. Pull the cord through and give it a gentle tug to settle it in place — one running

stitch made. Your needle will be on the inside of the shoe. Push the needle through the next hole in the upper, then through the next hole in the sole; pull the cord through, and give a gentle tug. Continue in this fashion, giving a gentle tug after each stitch you take. You want your stitches snug, but not so tight that the edge of the sole ripples. Work up the side of the heel cup, down the other side, and down the long side until you come to the hole near the curve of the toe where the second support row of holes begins.

You'll see a curved groove here, instead of a straight one. Your needle will come out toward the outside at the hole at the top of the curved groove. Stitch down past the curved groove to make the first stitch in the support row. Use your fingernail to guide the cord into the curved groove. Your needle should be on the inside of the shoe when you complete the curved stitch. Your next stitch will be into the first hole in the support row. Keep up your running stitch until you get to the end of the support row, then reverse your sewing direction and sew back toward the toe of the shoe. Your reversed stitches will fill in the empty grooves. When you've sewn the 6 stitches of the support row, you should end up at the very last hole of your uppers on that side, with your needle on the inside of the shoe.

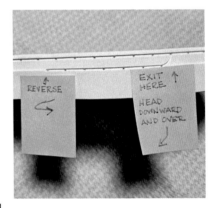

If you're not in this position, take an additional stitch on the inside of the shoe to help you get to where you need to be. Slip the needle through the first hole of the tongue, making sure that the lining side is facing toward the inside of the shoe. The edge of the upper and the edge of the tongue should be right next to each other, but not overlapping. If they do overlap a bit, make sure the uppers are next to the sole edge. Sew the tongue in the same way, with firm,

even running stitches through the holes you prepped in the fabric and the sole. When you get to the last hole in the tongue, your needle should be on the inside of the shoe. (Take an additional stitch if necessary.) Pass your needle through the first hole on the unsewn side of the upper and through the corresponding hole in the sole, down to and along the support row, reverse, and sew the remaining few running stitches. Notice that there are 7 holes on this side of the shoe. When you get back to where you began at the embossed arrow, reverse direction and sew around the shoe again, filling in the empty sections of the groove around the sole. You don't need to worry about the support row; those grooves should be completely filled. When you get back to the beginning, end your stitching inside the shoe, making an extra stitch if necessary. Tie off your cord, and trim the ends to about 2". Put a drop of seam sealant or permanent fabric glue on the knot.

Repeat this process for the left shoe.

Check to make sure all of your running stitches are snug and smooth.

Slip the insoles back inside the shoes. The insoles will remain in place without gluing, but you can use a bit of permanent flexible shoemaking glue to hold them in place if you'd like. If you need firmer or specialty insoles, use those instead of the insoles provided. You may have to trim commercial insoles a bit so that they fit smoothly in the sole bed. Use the provided insoles as a pattern to facilitate the trimming process. Trim just a bit at a time; you can always take a little more off, but once it's cut you can't put it back on!

Step 6: Show off your Happy Feet!

Lace your shoes as you'd like. Low versions of these sneakers use 45" laces; hi-tops use 60" laces. Lace them up, tie them in a perky bow, and show off your new shoes!

Supply Sources

Soles/insoles are available from the Chicago School of Shoemaking and Leather Arts online: www.chicagoschoolofshoemaking.com, as well as bucklebeebags.com.

Leatherworking cord is available in black, white and neutral colors from most large fabric and craft stores. For other color options, check big box online retailers.

To poke holes in soles, we use **cookie baking scribing tools**, available in the cake decorating aisle at craft stores or from online retailers, but any straight shafted stiletto will do. Avoid using a tool that increases in thickness, so you don't tear the soles.

We use **John James L 3/10 saddler's needles**, available at leatherworking and big box online retailers. A blunt needle is easier to use.

Leather punches are available at online big box retailers, craft, and hardware stores. A drill punch with changeable dies is a great tool for hole punches as well.

Eyelets are available at online retailers and leatherworking retailers. Usually, the eyelets are packaged in a kit with setting tools: punch, anvil, and setter. You'll need 32 eyelet sets for hi-tops; fewer for classic or ultra-low. Online retailers have wider color choices than most brick and mortar shops.

Your fingers will thank you for wearing a **hard thimble**. Pick one up at your favorite fabric store or local quilt shop.

For **bright shoelaces**, shop at online big box stores or at local discount or sporting goods stores. Remember to check the length of the laces! You'll need 60" laces for hi-tops, 45" for lower versions.

Made in United States
Orlando, FL
21 November 2024

54204406R00020